PLANES,
ROCKETS *and other*
FLYING MACHINES

Author:

Ian Graham was born in Belfast, Northern Ireland, in 1953. He studied applied physics at The City University, London, and took a postgraduate diploma in journalism at the same university, specializing in science and technology journalism. After four years as an editor of consumer electronics magazines, he became a freelance author and journalist. Since then, he has written more than one hundred children's non-fiction books and numerous magazine articles.

Series creator:

David Salariya was born in Dundee, Scotland, where he studied illustration and printmaking. He has illustrated a wide range of books and has created many new series of books for publishers in the U.K. and overseas. In 1989 he established The Salariya Book Company. He lives in Brighton with his wife, the illustrator Shirley Willis, and their son.

Artist:

Nick Hewetson was born in Surrey, England, in 1958. He was educated in Sussex at Brighton Technical School, and studied illustration at Eastbourne College of Art. He has illustrated a wide variety of children's books.

Editor:

Karen Barker Smith

Published in Great Britain in 2001 by
Hodder Wayland, an imprint of
Hodder Children's Books

A catalogue record for this book is available from
the British Library.

ISBN 0 7502 3629 9

Printed in China

Hodder Children's Books
A division of Hodder Headline Ltd
338 Euston Road, London NW1 3BH

Created, designed and produced by
THE SALARIYA BOOK COMPANY LTD
25 Marlborough Place,
Brighton BN1 1UB

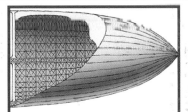

PLANES,
ROCKETS and other
FLYING MACHINES

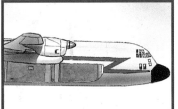

Written by
IAN GRAHAM

Illustrated by
NICK HEWETSON

Created and designed by
DAVID SALARIYA

HODDER
Wayland

An imprint of Hodder Children's Books

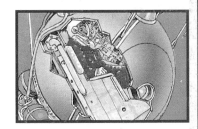

Contents

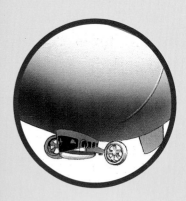

Dreams of Flight

A pilot made the wings of an early flying machine flap by moving his hands and feet. This machine (right) was one of many designed by Leonardo da Vinci in about 1500, but it was probably never built in his lifetime.

P eople have dreamed of flying like birds for thousands of years. Ancient myths and legends describe people who were able to fly with the help of bird-like wings. Early attempts to build machines to carry people into the sky were doomed to failure because they tried to copy the flapping action of birds. Their complicated mechanisms and strong wooden frames were far too heavy to fly using muscle power alone. The great Italian artist and engineer Leonardo da Vinci drew numerous flapping-wing designs for flying machines in the 15th century. They looked very impressive but were totally impractical. Success did not come until flapping wings were abandoned and fixed-wing gliders were studied instead. It took about 50 years of work by would-be aviators in Europe and the United States to find out how to control gliders in the air – how to make them climb and dive and turn this way or that, precisely as the pilot wanted. Then in 1903, two brothers in the United States added an engine and propellers to one of their gliders and created the first airplane, the Wright *Flyer*. The world would never be the same again.

Birds mastered the secret of flight millions of years before we did. Even now, after hundreds of years of scientific study and engineering advances, we still cannot build a machine that can match the skill, precision, and aerial grace of a bird in flight.

Cayley's glider

George Cayley made the first scientific study of flying machines by building model gliders. In 1849, one of his full-size gliders carried a small boy aloft. In 1853, his last glider (left) carried his coachman across a valley near his home at Brompton Hall in Yorkshire, England.

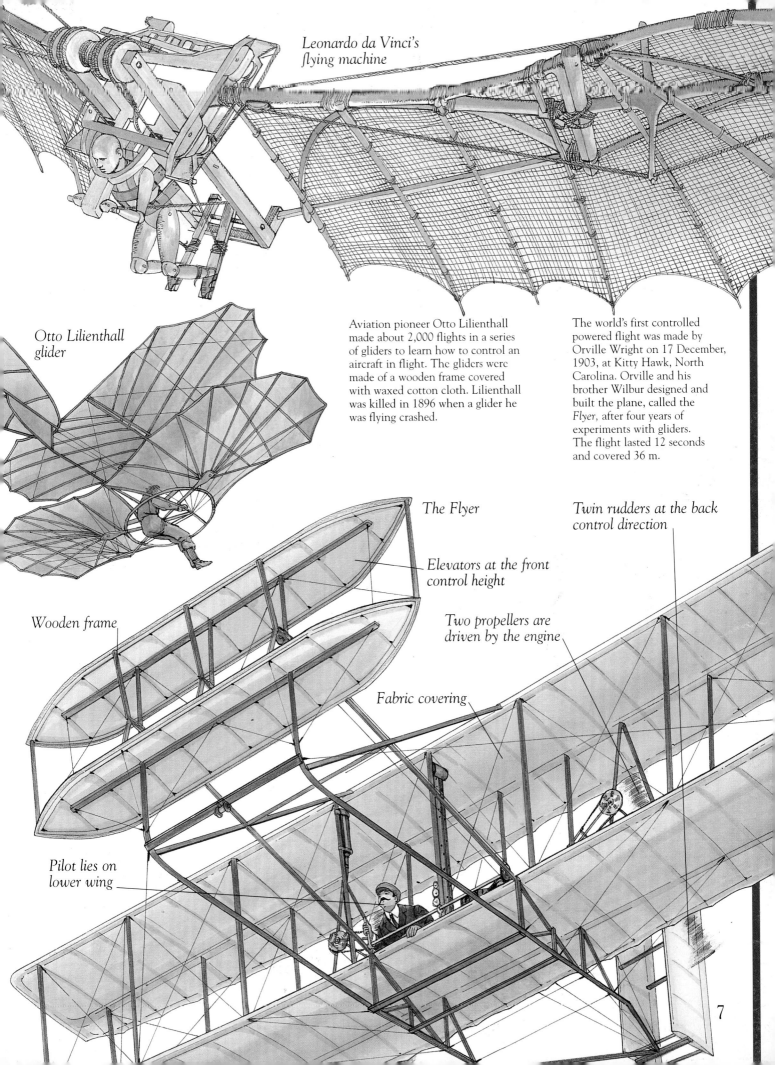

Leonardo da Vinci's flying machine

Otto Lilienthall glider

Aviation pioneer Otto Lilienthall made about 2,000 flights in a series of gliders to learn how to control an aircraft in flight. The gliders were made of a wooden frame covered with waxed cotton cloth. Lilienthall was killed in 1896 when a glider he was flying crashed.

The world's first controlled powered flight was made by Orville Wright on 17 December, 1903, at Kitty Hawk, North Carolina. Orville and his brother Wilbur designed and built the plane, called the *Flyer*, after four years of experiments with gliders. The flight lasted 12 seconds and covered 36 m.

The Flyer

Twin rudders at the back control direction

Elevators at the front control height

Two propellers are driven by the engine

Wooden frame

Fabric covering

Pilot lies on lower wing

The first non-stop flight across the Atlantic Ocean was made in 1919 by Captain John Alcock and Lieutenant Arthur Whitten Brown. They took off from Newfoundland in their World War I Vickers Vimy bomber and landed in Ireland 16 hours later.

Vickers Vimy

Trailblazers

Aviation pioneers have constantly pushed flying machines to their limits to make them fly farther, higher, and faster than ever. Courageous trailblazers often risked their lives to make historic flights. When Louis Blériot made the first flight across the English Channel in 1909, he had designed the plane himself and flew without any instruments at all. Many record-breaking flights were made just after World War I (1914–18) because there were plenty of ex-military pilots and planes available. Record-breaking 'route-proving' flights spanned the oceans and continents and prepared the way for the first passenger flights. The Atlantic Ocean was crossed in stages by seaplanes in May 1919, then non-stop in June 1919, and finally solo non-stop in 1927. Fierce competition between pilots and rivalry between plane-makers continually advanced aviation technology. World War II (1939–45) speeded up the development of jet-powered aircraft, rocket planes, and radar. The pace of invention and research has been so fast that only 66 years have passed between the world's first aeroplane flight and supersonic airliners.

Spirit of St. Louis

On 20 May, 1927, a Ryan NYP plane called the *Spirit of St. Louis*, weighed down with over 1,800 litres of fuel, struggled to take off from Long Island, New York. The plane had been converted to carry extra fuel for a special flight. The pilot, Charles Lindbergh, fought to stay awake until he landed 33 hours 39 minutes later in Paris. He became world-famous overnight as the first person to fly solo and non-stop across the North Atlantic Ocean.

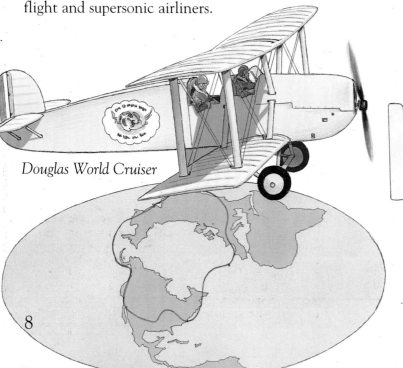

Douglas World Cruiser

Voyager

In 1924, two Douglas World Cruiser planes made the first round-the-world flight (left). They took 175 days and made 72 stops on the way. Sixty-two years later, in 1986, Dick Rutan and Jeana Yeager made the first non-stop round-the-world flight without re-fueling on the way. They were in the air for nine days, taking turns to fly their remarkable plane, *Voyager* (above).

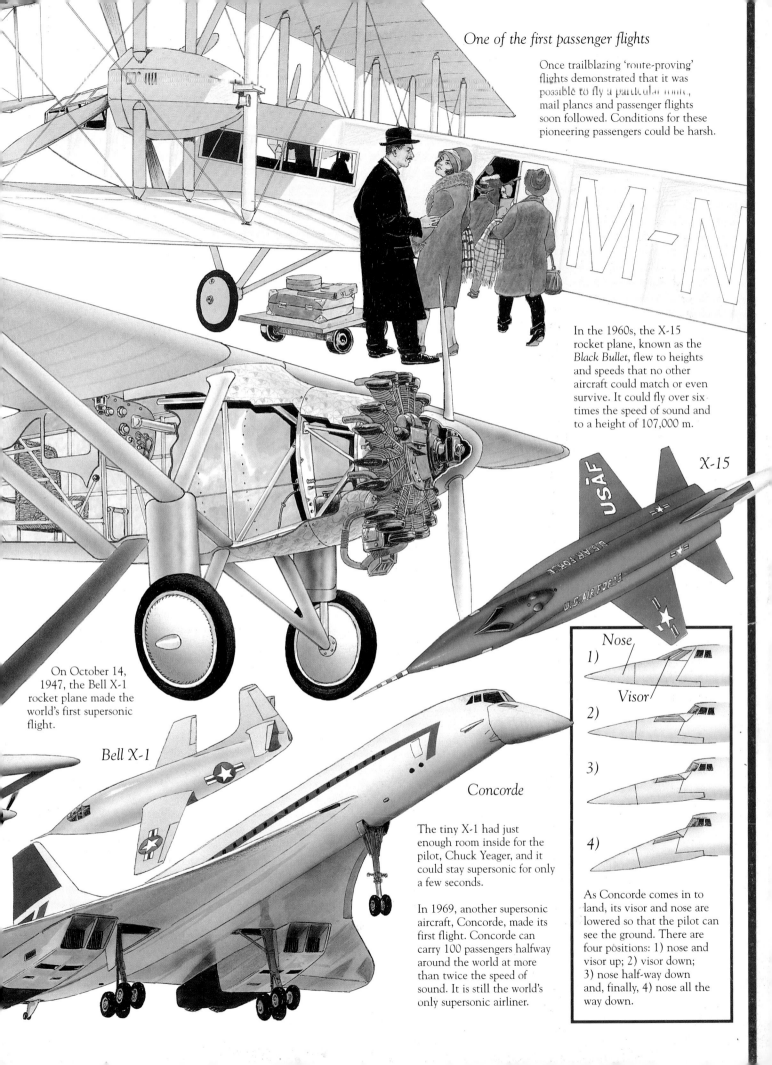

One of the first passenger flights

Once trailblazing 'route-proving' flights demonstrated that it was possible to fly a particular route, mail planes and passenger flights soon followed. Conditions for these pioneering passengers could be harsh.

In the 1960s, the X-15 rocket plane, known as the *Black Bullet*, flew to heights and speeds that no other aircraft could match or even survive. It could fly over six times the speed of sound and to a height of 107,000 m.

X-15

On October 14, 1947, the Bell X-1 rocket plane made the world's first supersonic flight.

Bell X-1

Concorde

The tiny X-1 had just enough room inside for the pilot, Chuck Yeager, and it could stay supersonic for only a few seconds.

In 1969, another supersonic aircraft, Concorde, made its first flight. Concorde can carry 100 passengers halfway around the world at more than twice the speed of sound. It is still the world's only supersonic airliner.

Nose

1)

Visor

2)

3)

4)

As Concorde comes in to land, its visor and nose are lowered so that the pilot can see the ground. There are four positions: 1) nose and visor up; 2) visor down; 3) nose half-way down and, finally, 4) nose all the way down.

Planes for War

Aeroplanes went to war for the first time during World War I. At first, they were used only to spy on enemy positions. Then pilots started dropping bombs by hand from their planes, and other small, fast planes were sent to fight them. World War I fighters like the Sopwith Camel were made of a wooden frame covered by fabric, but by the 1930s all-metal monoplanes had replaced them. World War II fighters like the Messerschmitt Bf-109 and Hawker Hurricane could reach 500 kilometres per hour (kph), and by the end of the war, jet fighters were introduced.

Fighters and bombers are the two main types of warplanes in service today. In addition, strike aircraft attack ground targets, interceptors stop enemy planes getting through to their targets, reconnaissance planes spy on the enemy, and electronic warfare planes jam enemy radar and communications. Fighter-bombers like the Lockheed F-16 Fighting Falcon can serve as both fighters and bombers. Multi-role aeroplanes like the Eurofighter EFA 2000 work as fighters, strike planes, and bombers. The biggest bombers are long-range strategic bombers like the giant Boeing B-52. A spy plane, the Lockheed SR-71 Blackbird, holds the world air speed record: 3,529 kph. The most advanced warplanes are stealth planes. Their strange shape helps them avoid being detected by enemy radar.

Fokker Triplane

The fighter pilot's job has not changed since the first fighters took to the skies during World War I: move into position to shoot down an enemy plane while avoiding becoming a target yourself. Modern fighter pilots still practise dogfights with each other to prepare for combat.

Sopwith Camel

Sopwith Camels were armed with machine guns and could fly at about 200 kph.

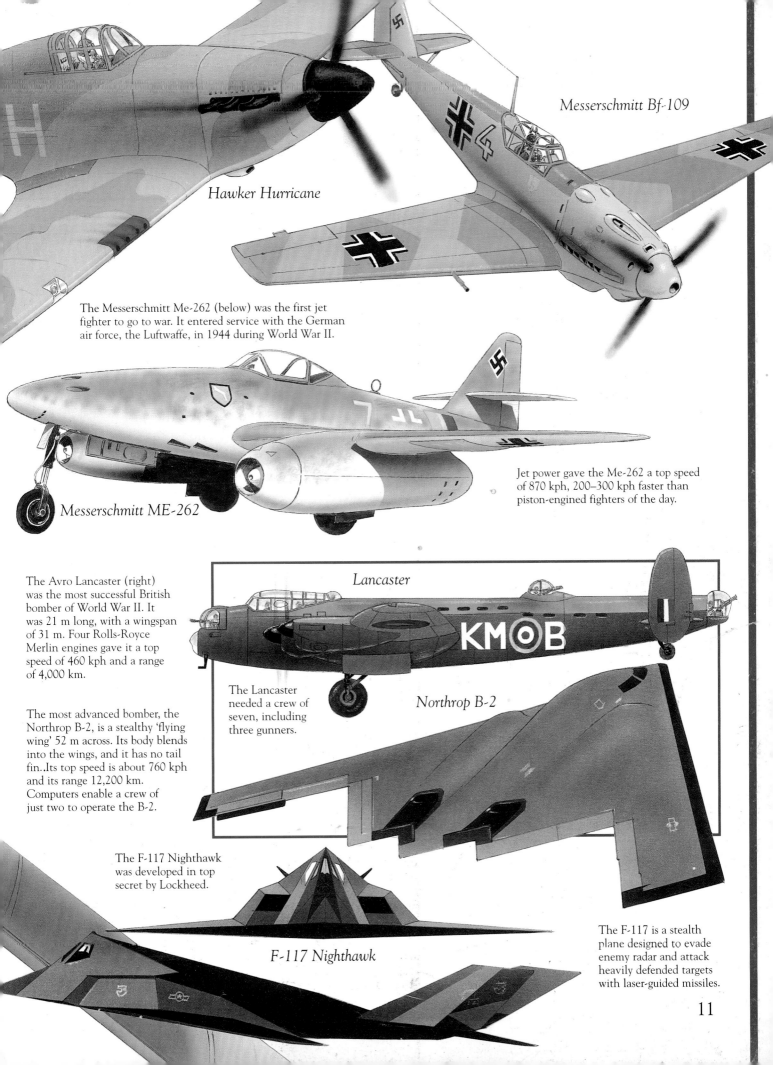

Messerschmitt Bf-109

Hawker Hurricane

The Messerschmitt Me-262 (below) was the first jet fighter to go to war. It entered service with the German air force, the Luftwaffe, in 1944 during World War II.

Messerschmitt ME-262

Jet power gave the Me-262 a top speed of 870 kph, 200–300 kph faster than piston-engined fighters of the day.

The Avro Lancaster (right) was the most successful British bomber of World War II. It was 21 m long, with a wingspan of 31 m. Four Rolls-Royce Merlin engines gave it a top speed of 460 kph and a range of 4,000 km.

Lancaster

The Lancaster needed a crew of seven, including three gunners.

The most advanced bomber, the Northrop B-2, is a stealthy 'flying wing' 52 m across. Its body blends into the wings, and it has no tail fin..Its top speed is about 760 kph and its range 12,200 km. Computers enable a crew of just two to operate the B-2.

Northrop B-2

The F-117 Nighthawk was developed in top secret by Lockheed.

F-117 Nighthawk

The F-117 is a stealth plane designed to evade enemy radar and attack heavily defended targets with laser-guided missiles.

11

Balloons and Airships

The first manned flight was made 120 years before the first aeroplane was built. It was achieved using a hot-air balloon, a craft that floated upward because the hot air inside it was lighter than the surrounding air. The air was heated by a fire, burning on a platform slung underneath the balloon. Flying in an early hot-air balloon was risky because balloons were often set alight by sparks from their fires. Modern hot-air balloons are made from flameproof materials. Balloons travel wherever the wind blows them, but airships can be steered.

The German Zeppelin LZ 129, the *Hindenburg*, is pictured below manoeuvering toward its mooring mast at the end of a flight. Along with its sister ship, the *Graf Zeppelin II*, it was the biggest airship ever built. It was 245 m long and 41 m across. Starting in 1936, it carried up to 50 passengers at a time across the Atlantic Ocean between Germany and the United States. A typical flight from Frankfurt to Lakehurst, New Jersey, took about 65 hours. The *Hindenburg* was so popular that it was always fully booked.

The first manned flight in a hot-air balloon was made on 21 November, 1783. The balloon (below), made by the Montgolfier brothers, carried two men aloft over Paris for 25 minutes.

D-LZ129

Engines

Passenger decks

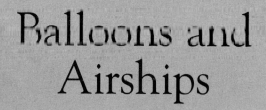

Montgolfier balloon

In 1852, Frenchman Henri Giffard suspended a steam engine under a long, thin hydrogen balloon. The engine drove a propeller. On 24 September, Giffard took off from Paris in his machine, flying 27 km on the world's first powered airship flight.

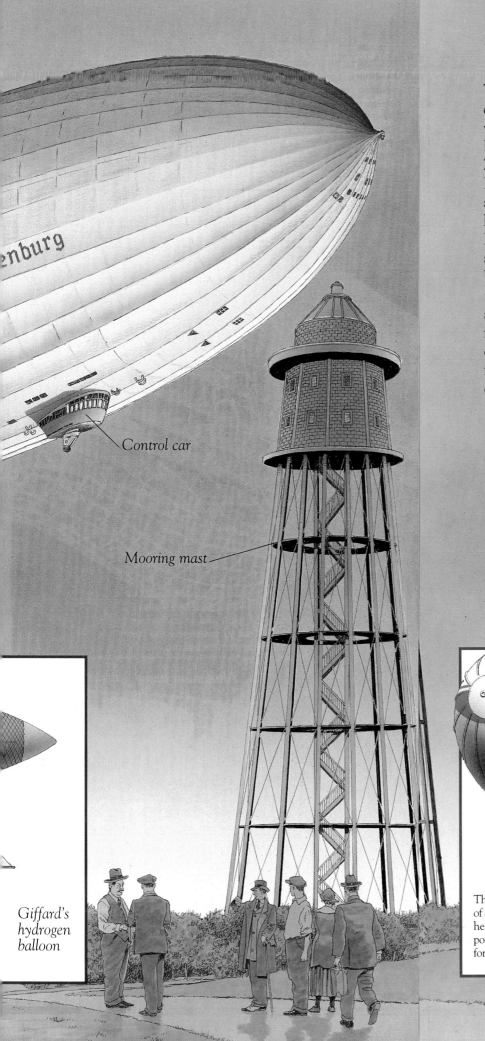

The majestic German Zeppelins had a dangerous weakness: they were filled with hydrogen gas. Hydrogen is the lightest gas of all, so it allowed the Zeppelins to lift the maximum weight. But it is also highly flammable. If a hydrogen airship caught fire, its hydrogen gas burned uncontrollably. Helium, a safer gas used in all modern airships, was available only in the United States and denied to Germany in the 1930s. Several hydrogen airships had already been destroyed by fire, but when the mighty *Hindenburg* crashed to the ground in flames in front of news cameras, it marked the end of the golden age of airship travel.

Control car

Mooring mast

Giffard's hydrogen balloon

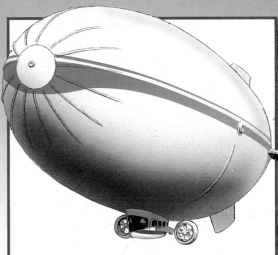

The Skyship 500 is typical of the new generation of modern airships. Its envelope is filled with safe helium gas. Two Porsche car engines provide the power, and there is enough room inside the gondola for a crew of two plus up to eight passengers.

15

Special Planes

ircraft can carry out an amazing range of activities. As well as carrying passengers, planes are used to spray crops, fight fires, carry cargo, fly security patrols, work as air ambulances, and compete in air contests. Aircraft are often designed and built specially to do a particular job. Cargo planes are built with large holds, and fire-fighting planes have tanks that can hold thousands of gallons of water. Aerobatic planes are immensely strong to withstand the stress of tumbling through the sky. Seaplanes and flying boats can land on water. Other aircraft may be converted for a specific task. Planes used for security work are equipped with night-vision aids, while air ambulances are supplied with stretchers and medical equipment. Air races often feature aircraft that were originally World War II fighters, like the P-51 Mustang.

Junkers Ju 52/3m

Lockheed C-130 Hercules

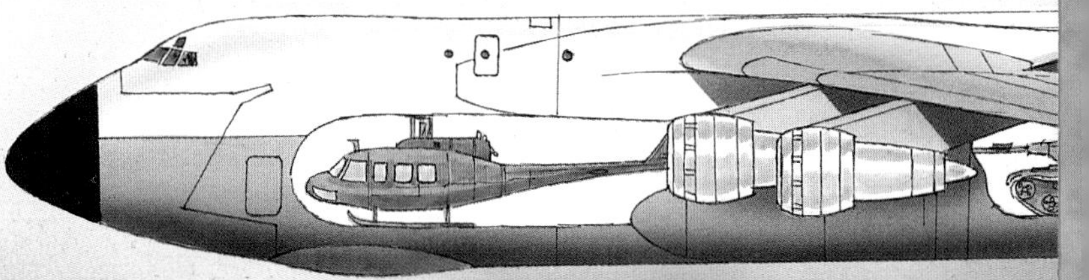

Lockheed C-5 Galaxy

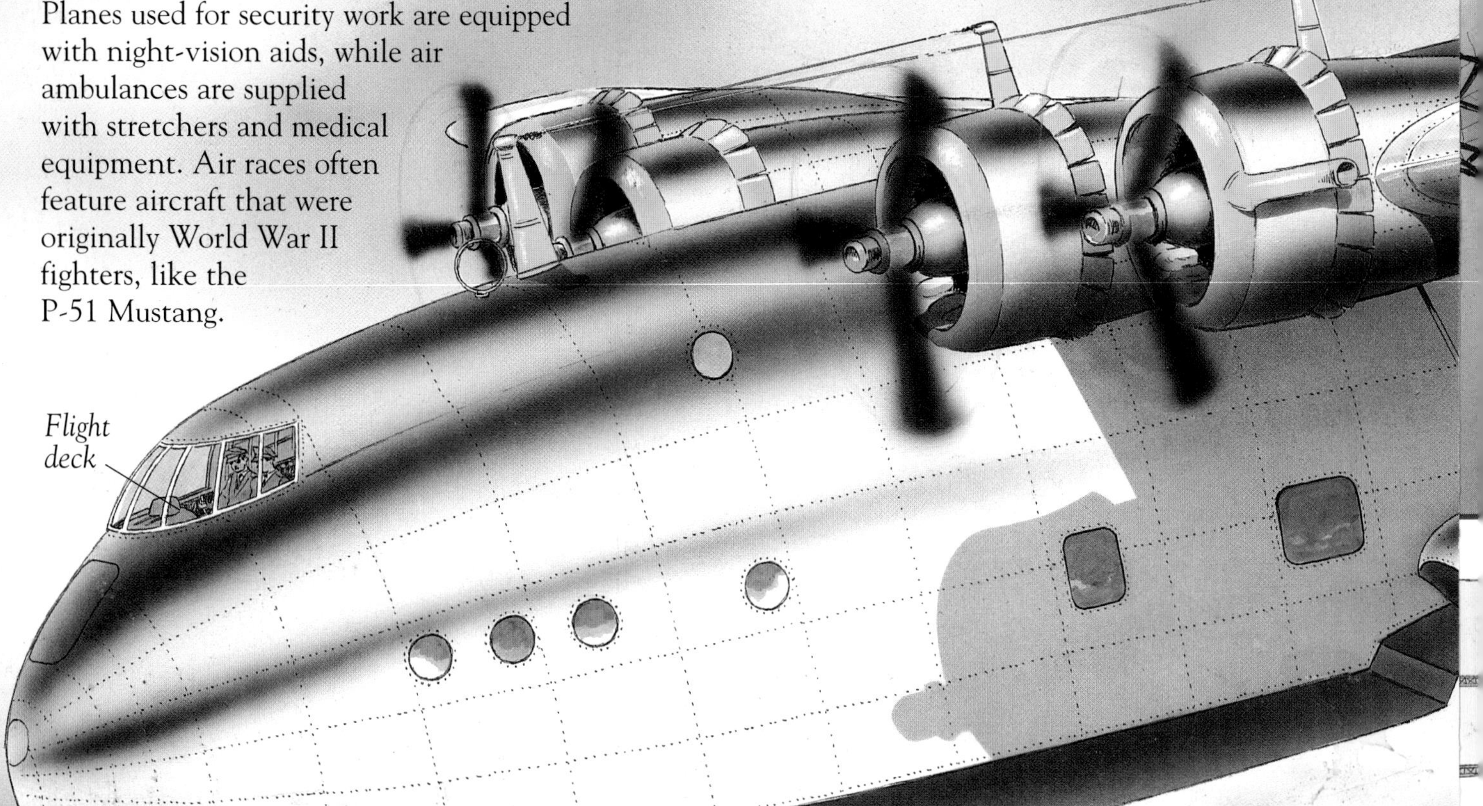

Flight deck

Shorts S23 flying boat

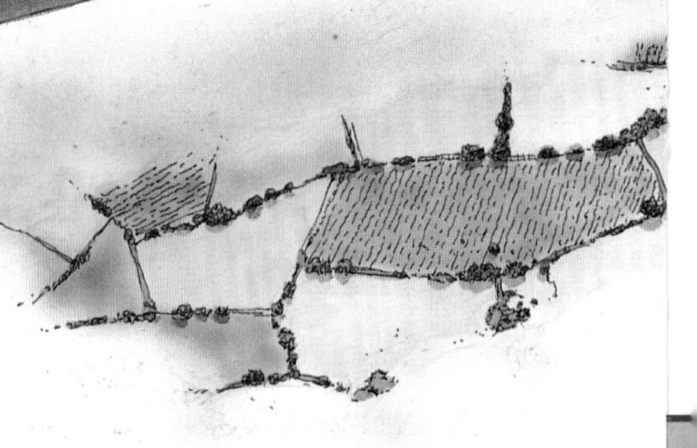

The biggest aircraft of all are military transport planes. During World War II, the Junkers Ju 52/3m was the standard German transport plane. It had a wingspan of 29 m and could carry 17 soldiers at 260 kph. The Lockheed C-130 Hercules, still in service, has a wingspan of 40 m and can carry 16,000 kg of cargo at 600 kph.

The biggest transport plane of all, the Lockheed C-5 Galaxy, has a wingspan of 68 m and can carry a payload of almost 120,000 kg, including tanks and helicopters, at 900 kph.

Private jets (below) are small airliners that are used as air taxis by busy people who do not want to wait for scheduled flights. They carry between six and 20 passengers. Some private jets are furnished like offices.

The Canadair CL-415 (above) is a fire-fighting plane designed to deal with forest fires in Canada. It fills its water tanks by skimming along the surfaces of lakes. Without stopping, it scoops up 6,000 litres of water in only 12 seconds. Then, as it flies over the fire, doors in the bottom of the tanks open and the water drops out.

Helicopters

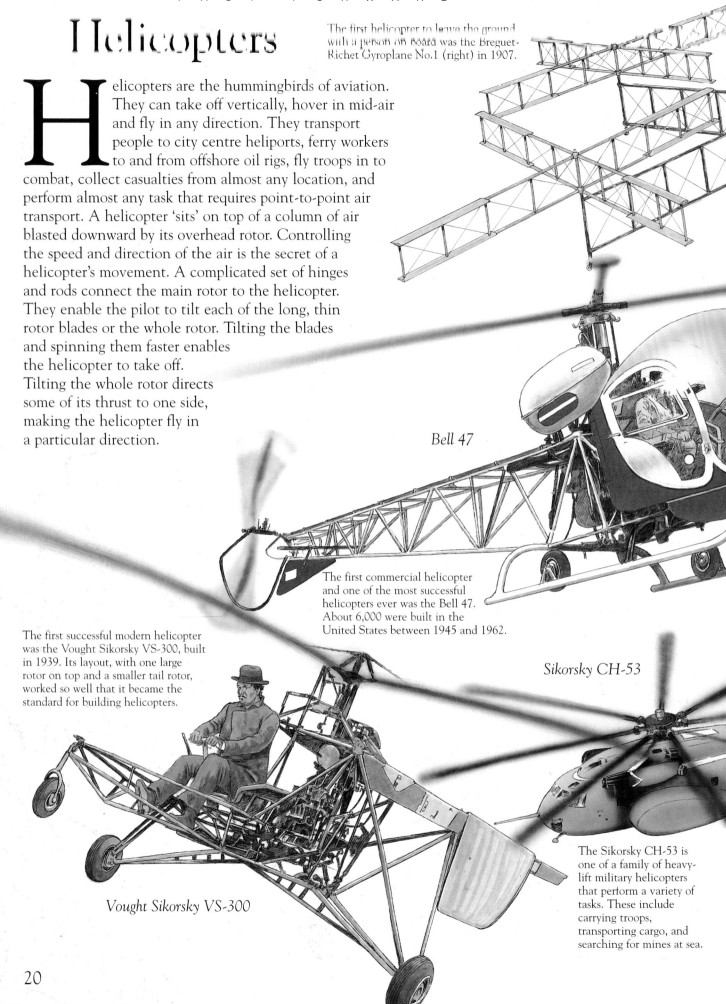

The first helicopter to leave the ground with a person on board was the Breguet-Richet Gyroplane No.1 (right) in 1907.

Helicopters are the hummingbirds of aviation. They can take off vertically, hover in mid-air and fly in any direction. They transport people to city centre heliports, ferry workers to and from offshore oil rigs, fly troops in to combat, collect casualties from almost any location, and perform almost any task that requires point-to-point air transport. A helicopter 'sits' on top of a column of air blasted downward by its overhead rotor. Controlling the speed and direction of the air is the secret of a helicopter's movement. A complicated set of hinges and rods connect the main rotor to the helicopter. They enable the pilot to tilt each of the long, thin rotor blades or the whole rotor. Tilting the blades and spinning them faster enables the helicopter to take off. Tilting the whole rotor directs some of its thrust to one side, making the helicopter fly in a particular direction.

Bell 47

The first commercial helicopter and one of the most successful helicopters ever was the Bell 47. About 6,000 were built in the United States between 1945 and 1962.

The first successful modern helicopter was the Vought Sikorsky VS-300, built in 1939. Its layout, with one large rotor on top and a smaller tail rotor, worked so well that it became the standard for building helicopters.

Sikorsky CH-53

Vought Sikorsky VS-300

The Sikorsky CH-53 is one of a family of heavy-lift military helicopters that perform a variety of tasks. These include carrying troops, transporting cargo, and searching for mines at sea.

Breguet-Richet Gyroplane No.1

Bell UH-1 Iroquois

CH-47 Chinook

Helicopters were used extensively during the U.S. military involvement in the Vietnam War (1965–1975). The Bell UH-1 Iroquois carried troops and evacuated casualties. The Boeing Vertol CH-47 Chinook was the main heavy-lift helicopter of the war, transporting up to 40 troops or eight tonnes of cargo every flight.

The McDonnell Douglas AH-64 Apache is a formidable attack helicopter. Its job is to attack armoured vehicles, especially tanks. The Apache is heavily armed with a machine gun under its nose and laser-guided anti-tank missiles.

AH-64 Apache

Airliners and Airports

In the early years of passenger air travel, flights could be uncomfortable journeys. The first airliners were often converted World War I bombers. They were unreliable and cold because they weren't insulated. They were also so noisy that airlines offered passengers earplugs to wear on some flights! The planes often took off from grass airfields, where tents or wooden sheds served as passenger terminals. In the 1930s, as the popularity of air travel grew and more airlines were created, a new generation of purpose-built, all-metal airliners like the Boeing 247 and Douglas DC-1 were introduced.

The Boeing 247 flew at a height of about 5,500 m, only half that of a Boeing 747 jumbo jet today. A flight at that height, among the clouds and storms, could be very bumpy.

Boeing 247

Airliners like the Boeing 247, which was introduced in 1933, heralded a new level of comfort and service in air travel. Its passengers were taken care of by the first airline stewardesses, who were often trained nurses.

In 1930, Boeing Air Transport employed the very first airline stewardess, Ellen Church (left), to look after its passengers' needs.

A Boeing 247 (above) at a typical 1930s airport. Compared to a modern airport, there was little or no security. There were no jets – jet airliners were not common until the 1950s – and the planes were smaller and slower than airliners today.

The Boeing 247, the first modern airliner, was 16.5 m long and had a wingspan of 22.6 m. It could carry ten passengers along with a stewardess at a speed of 275 kph.

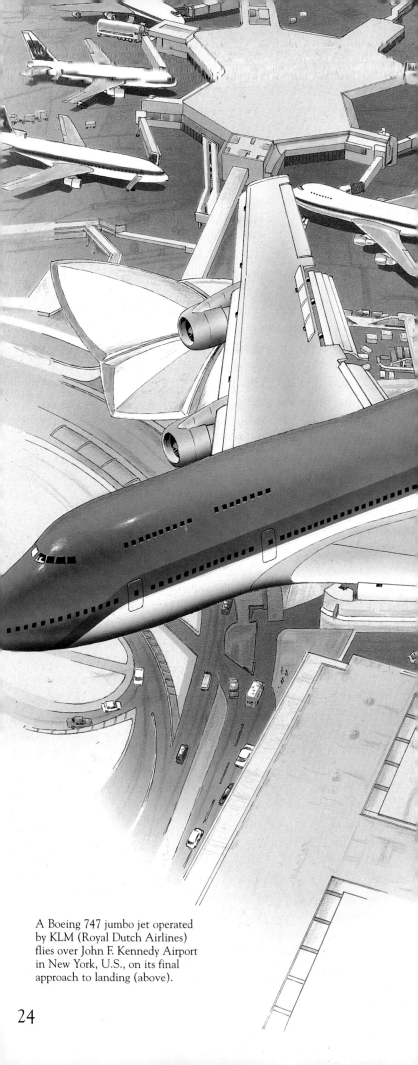

A Boeing 747 jumbo jet operated
by KLM (Royal Dutch Airlines)
flies over John F. Kennedy Airport
in New York, U.S., on its final
approach to landing (above).

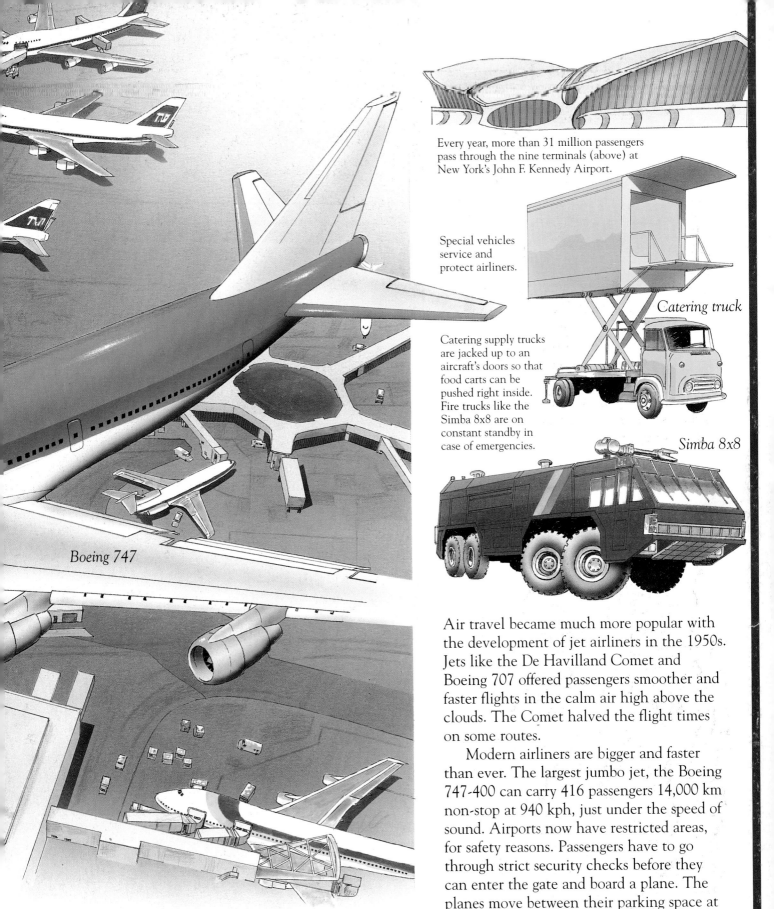

Every year, more than 31 million passengers pass through the nine terminals (above) at New York's John F. Kennedy Airport.

Special vehicles service and protect airliners.

Catering truck

Catering supply trucks are jacked up to an aircraft's doors so that food carts can be pushed right inside. Fire trucks like the Simba 8x8 are on constant standby in case of emergencies.

Simba 8x8

Boeing 747

KLM is the oldest airline in the world that is still operating. John F. Kennedy Airport was originally called Idlewild. It was renamed John F. Kennedy in 1963 in honour of the U.S. president who was assassinated that year.

Air travel became much more popular with the development of jet airliners in the 1950s. Jets like the De Havilland Comet and Boeing 707 offered passengers smoother and faster flights in the calm air high above the clouds. The Comet halved the flight times on some routes.

Modern airliners are bigger and faster than ever. The largest jumbo jet, the Boeing 747-400 can carry 416 passengers 14,000 km non-stop at 940 kph, just under the speed of sound. Airports now have restricted areas, for safety reasons. Passengers have to go through strict security checks before they can enter the gate and board a plane. The planes move between their parking space at the terminals and the runways on a network of taxiways.

Spacecraft

On 4 October, 1957, a metal ball 58 cm in diameter was blasted into orbit around Earth. It was *Sputnik 1*, the world's first artificial satellite. The only type of vehicle that was powerful enough to launch satellites and capable of working in the airless vacuum of space was the rocket. The United States and the former Soviet Union raced against each other to launch bigger satellites and to reach the planets with space probes. The Soviet Union won the race to launch the first human being into space. The United States progressed from one-man *Mercury* space projects to two-man *Gemini* missions to learn how to manoeuver spacecraft. Then they developed the three-man *Apollo* spacecraft and the giant *Saturn V* rocket to take it to the moon. With *Apollo 11*, the United States succeeded in landing the first men on the moon, in 1969.

Command and service module (CSM)

The *Apollo* lunar module descended to the moon using its rocket engine to slow down for a gentle landing. After up to three days on the surface, the lunar excursion module (LEM) blasted off, using its base as a launchpad, and returned to the orbiting CSM.

Lunar excursion module (LEM)

Yuri Gagarin

Main rocket engine nozzle

The first person to leave Earth and travel into space was Yuri Gagarin, a Soviet pilot. On 12 April, 1961, he made one orbit of the Earth in his *Vostok 1* space capsule and then landed safely back in the Soviet Union.

Vostok 1

Lunar module

Moon buggy

Parachute compartment

Main instrument panel

Command module

Crew compartment

Quad thruster

Service module

Apollo astronauts travelled to the moon in the *Apollo* CSM (Command and Service Module). For most of the journey it was docked with the Lunar Excursion Module (LEM). The astronauts lived in the tiny Command Module and the Service Module supplied them with oxygen to breathe and electrical power. It also contained the rocket engine that sent them on their way to the moon and brought them back to Earth again. Once the spacecraft was safely in orbit around the moon, two of the three astronauts floated through the docking tunnel into the LEM, undocked from the CSM, and descended to the moon.

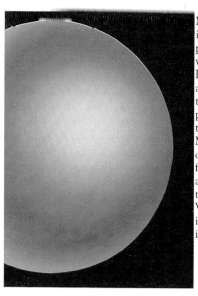

Mars, the red planet, is the second closest planet to us – it comes within 56 million km of Earth. Its day is only a few minutes longer than ours, and it has polar ice caps. But there the similarity ends. Mars is half the size of Earth and is farther from the sun – its average surface temperature is -23°C. We could not breathe in its atmosphere, as it is 95% carbon dioxide.

Mars module of the future

Space shuttle

A space shuttle stands by at a safe
distance as a spacecraft blasts out of
Earth's orbit on its way to Mars (above).
A future Mars craft may be built in orbit from
parts carried there by dozens, perhaps hundreds, of space shuttle flights.
For the astronauts on board the giant craft, the journey to the red planet will
take at least nine months. To save weight, they may land on Mars with empty
fuel tanks. The vital fuel they will need for their take-off and return to Earth
could be made from the Martian atmosphere.

1. The space shuttle blasts off
from the Kennedy Space Center
in Florida.
2. At a height of 44 km, the solid
rocket boosters fall away.
3. At 113 km, the external fuel
tank falls away.
4. The orbiter craft continues
into orbit.
5. The payload bay doors open
to launch satellites or bring
faulty ones in for repair.
6. The orbital rocket engines
fire to slow the orbiter so that
it begins to fall back to Earth.
7. The orbiter glows as it
re-enters the atmosphere.
8. The orbiter glides down
through the atmosphere.
9. Wheels down, the orbiter
touches down on the Kennedy
Space Center's runway.

Glossary

Aviator
Another name for a pilot.

Dogfight
An air battle between fighter-planes.

Elevators
Panels in a plane's tail that are tilted up or down by the pilot to swing the plane's nose up or down.

Envelope
The fabric or other material that covers an airship's gas bags.

Flight deck
The part of an aircraft where the pilots sit.

Flying boat
An aeroplane with a boat-shaped body and floats under its wings that can land on water.

Jet fighter
A military aeroplane powered by one or more jet engines.

Lift
The upward force created by a plane's wings, a helicopter's rotor blades, or the gas inside a balloon or airship.

Monoplane
An aeroplane with one set of wings.

Orbit
The path that a satellite or spacecraft follows as it circles a planet.

Payload
Another name for cargo.

Propeller
An angled blade, which spins to pull a plane through the air.

Radar
RAdio Detection And Ranging. A system for locating objects that are too far away to see. It works by bouncing radio waves off them and measuring the time for the reflected waves to return.

Range
The maximum distance an aircraft can fly without having to re-fuel.

Reconnaissance
Obtaining information about the position, activities, etc. of an enemy.

Rotor
A set of rotating blades used by helicopters.

Rudder
A panel in an aircraft's tail fin that is swivelled to one side or the other by the pilot to turn the aircraft's nose to the left or right.

Satellite
An object, such as a spacecraft or a moon, that orbits another object, such as a planet.

Seaplane
An aeroplane that can land on water using floats instead of wheels.

Stealth plane
A warplane that is designed to be difficult for an enemy to find by radar. Its shape and covering of special materials stops the enemy's radar waves from being reflected back strongly.

Supersonic
Faster than the speed of sound.

Wingspan
The distance between a plane's wingtips.

Plane and Rocket Facts

The Wright brothers steered their aircraft by pulling wires to bend the ends of the wings, called wing-warping.

Every aircraft is acted on by four forces in different directions – weight (downward), lift (upward), thrust (forward), and drag (backward).

The special shape of an aeroplane's wings and a helicopter's rotor blades, curved on top and flat underneath, is called an aerofoil.

The supersonic airliner Concorde is heated by the air it hurtles through at twice the speed of sound, so that it expands by 20-25 cm during each flight.

The white trails left by high-flying planes are ice crystals. Hydrogen from the engines reacts with oxygen in the air, making water, which instantly freezes. The trails are called contrails.

The world's biggest helicopter is the Russian Mil Mi-26. Its main rotor is 33 m across, and it has a maximum take-off weight of 56,000 kg.

The world airspeed record for helicopters is 400.87 kph, set by a British Westland Lynx in 1986.

The Harrier 'jump jet' can take off vertically and hover like a helicopter by directing its jet's four nozzles downward.

A fully loaded Boeing 747-400 jumbo jet can weigh as much as 395 tonnes at take-off.

An airliner's tyres are changed about every 200 landings.

When the space shuttle re-enters Earth's atmosphere, it is flying at approximately 25 times the speed of sound.

If all four of a jumbo jet's engines failed, it could glide more than 110 km in any direction before having to land.

During a flight, the air outside a jumbo jet's window can be as cold as -50°C.

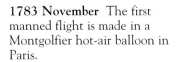

Chronology

1783 November The first manned flight is made in a Montgolfier hot-air balloon in Paris.

1853 Sir George Cayley's coachman is the first person to fly in a glider, built by Cayley.

1896 German aviation pioneer Otto Lilienthall is killed when one of his gliders crashes.

1903 The Wright brothers make the first powered, controlled flight in an aeroplane.

1919 Alcock and Brown make the first non-stop crossing of the Atlantic Ocean in a Vickers Vimy bomber.

1926 Robert Goddard launches the first liquid-fuelled rocket.

1927 Charles Lindbergh flies solo and non-stop across the North Atlantic Ocean in his plane, the *Spirit of St. Louis*.

1937 The *Hindenburg* Zeppelin crashes to the ground in flames while landing at Lakehurst, New Jersey, in the United States.

1939 Igor Sikorsky designs the first practical and successful helicopter, the VS-300.

1947 Charles "Chuck" Yeager makes the first supersonic flight in the Bell X-1 experimental rocket plane.

1952 The first jet airliner, the De Havilland Comet, enters service.

1957 October *Sputnik 1*, launched by the Soviet Union, is the world's first artificial satellite.

1957 November *Sputnik 2* carries the first living creature, a dog called Laika, into space.

1961 April Yuri Gagarin is the first human being to leave Earth and travel into space.

1961 May Alan Sheppard becomes the first U.S. astronaut.

1962 John Glenn becomes the first U.S. astronaut to orbit the Earth, in his "Friendship 7" *Mercury* capsule.

1963 Valentina Tereshkova becomes the first woman in space on board *Vostok 6*.

1968 December The Tupolev Tu-144 supersonic airliner makes its maiden flight.

1968 December Human beings circle the moon for the first time. They are Frank Borman, Jim Lovell, and Fred Haise: the crew of *Apollo 8*.

1969 February The Boeing 747 jumbo jet makes its maiden flight. It is the world's first 'wide-body' commercial air transport.

1969 March The supersonic airliner Concorde makes its maiden flight.

1969 July Neil Armstrong is the first person to walk on the moon, closely followed by Edwin "Buzz" Aldrin, while Michael Collins circles the moon. They are the crew of *Apollo 11*.

1970 January The Boeing 747 jumbo jet enters service with U.S. airline Pan Am.

1970 April *Apollo 13* fails to land on the moon because of an explosion in the spacecraft. The crew returns to Earth safely.

1970 December The Soviet Union lands the first space probe, *Venera 7*, on the surface of Venus.

1971 The Soviet space station *Salyut 1* is launched.

1972 August Don Cameron and Mark Yarry make the first hot-air balloon crossing of the Swiss Alps.

1972 December The final *Apollo* mission, *Apollo 17*, lands on the moon.

1973 The U.S. space station *Skylab* is launched but is severely

damaged by vibration. It was in use for only six months of its six years in orbit.

1976 January The supersonic airliner Concorde enters service.

1976 July The Lockheed SR-71 Blackbird spyplane sets a world airspeed record of 3,529 kph.

1976 July and **September** Two U.S. *Viking* spacecraft land on the planet Mars. They search for life but find none.

1977 *Voyager 1* and *Voyager 2* launch on their grand tour of the solar system. They send back breathtaking photographs of the planets and their moons but later leave our solar system and now are no longer in contact.

1978 *Double Eagle II*, piloted by Ben Abruzzo, Maxie Anderson, and Larry Newman, is the first gas balloon to cross the Atlantic Ocean.

1981 The U.S. space shuttle makes its first flight.

1983 The last of the Soviet *Salyut* space stations, *Salyut 7*, is launched.

1986 February The Soviet Union launches the *Mir* space station.

1986 August A Westland Lynx piloted by John Eggington and Derek Clews sets the world airspeed record for helicopters of 400.87 kph.

1986 December Jeana Yeager and Dick Rutan make the first non-stop flight around the world in their specially built plane *Voyager*.

1988 Per Lindstrand reaches the greatest altitude for a hot-air balloon: 19,811 m.

1999 Bertrand Piccard and Brian Jones make the first non-stop round-the-world flight by hot-air balloon in the *Breitling Orbiter III*.

Index